ONE *Flame*

GARY SMALLEY

TYNDALE HOUSE
PUBLISHERS, INC.
WHEATON, ILLINOIS

Visit Tyndale's exciting Web site at www.tyndale.com

One Flame

Copyright © 2002 by Smalley Publishing Group, LLC. All rights reserved.

Cover photograph copyright © 2001 Tyndale House Publishers. All rights reserved.

Interior images for chapters 3 and 6 © 2001 by Scott Barrow. All rights reserved.

Photographs for chapters four and five © Photodisc. All rights reserved.

Author photo by Jim Lersch. All rights reserved.

Published in association with the literary agency of Alive Communications, Inc., 7680 Goddard Street, Suite 200, Colorado Springs, CO 80920.

This book is adapted from chapters 10 and 11 of Gary Smalley's *Food and Love* (Wheaton, Ill.: Tyndale House, 2001). Used by permission.

Designed by Timothy R. Botts

Edited by Lynn Vanderzalm

Unless otherwise indicated, all Scripture quotations are taken from the *Holy Bible*, New Living Translation, copyright © 1996. Used by permission of Tyndale House Publishers, Inc., Wheaton, Illinois 60189. All rights reserved.

Scripture quotations marked NIV are taken from the *Holy Bible*, New International Version®. NIV®. Copyright © 1973, 1978, 1984 by International Bible Society. Used by permission of Zondervan Publishing House. All rights reserved.

Library of Congress Cataloging-in-Publication Data

Smalley, Gary.
    One flame / Gary Smalley.
        p. cm.
Book is adapted from chapters 10 and 11 of the author's Food and love.
    ISBN 0-8423-6564-8 (hc)
1. Marriage. 2. Marriage—Religious aspects—Christianity.   I. Smalley, Gary. Food and love.
II. Title.
HQ734 .S6864 2002
306.81—dc21   2001005916

Printed in the United States of America

07   06   05   04   03   02
8   7   6   5   4   3   2   1

To Norma Jean,
who is truly the wind
beneath my wings

CONTENTS

ACKNOWLEDGMENTS

My deepest thanks goes to my wife, Norma, to whom I have been married for nearly four decades. Norma, your love, faithfulness, and insight have taught me so much about oneness. Without your grace and patience, our flame would have flickered long ago. You reflect God's grace and love for me every day. Thank you.

A heartfelt thanks goes to our children and their spouses: Greg and Erin, Mike and Amy, and Kari and Roger. You and your marriages are a source of deep joy for me. Thank you for honoring each other and valuing the oneness God has given you.

I thank Karen Kingsbury, who once again has collaborated with me. This book is adapted from *Food and Love,* another book we worked on together. Karen, you know that I am one of your most enthusiastic fans. Your novels move me to tears and have left a deep impact on my life. I look forward to working on several novels with you in the coming years.

Thanks to Greg Johnson, my agent. You have an amazing and

creative ability to put together contracts that will glorify God. Thanks for shepherding me through what feels like a second publishing life.

Thanks also to the Tyndale team: Ron Beers, Ken Petersen, and Lynn Vanderzalm. You have a very special way of listening and hearing my heart's passions.

CHAPTER 1

Is the
flame
still
burning?

EW THINGS are more beautiful than the flame of a unity candle burning brightly during a wedding ceremony. It is a picture of the truth that in marriage, the two become one.

Oneness is the strength of marriage, a safe harbor. It is the place where the couple is stronger than either partner is separately.

If you lit the flame of a unity candle during your wedding, the question to you is this: Is your flame of oneness still burning brightly?

In other words, do you feel a deep sense of oneness in your marriage today? Do you feel safe and satisfied with a deep intimacy that you both enjoy? Are you as happily married as you would like to be? I truly believe that this little book can bring you the simplest but greatest truth I've ever learned about how couples become very satisfied and stay in love.

The Amazing Secret of the Unity Candle

If you used the unity candle in your wedding, did you understand what you were doing? Norma and I used it, but I'm not certain I understood the meaning behind the lighting ceremony at the time.

Now that I do understand it, I believe that within this

simple ceremony lie the secrets to a better marriage. The greatest secret of all is oneness: the ability to let go of our single status and join together with our spouse for all of life. By the end of this book, I believe you'll understand what I have learned about the unity-candle ceremony's amazing value.

The lack of oneness causes many people to suffer in relationships that are neither rewarding nor uplifting. The problem is that these people are more devoted to their own flame of self than to the one flame they share together as a married couple.

When we are focused more on ourselves than on what's good for our marriage, conflicts often arise. These conflicts can drain us if we don't know how to handle them.

Conflicts are inevitable. They arise even when we do not invite them. Take a look at how different my wife, Norma, and I are. Before we knew how to use the secret behind the unity-candle ceremony, this event could have been one more conflict to blow out our "light."

A Hot Time in the Smalley Home

One day I was getting ready for a trip and wanted to do a bit of laundry before I packed. When I opened the washer, I saw that some of Norma's clothing was in the bottom, waiting to be placed in the dryer. I took out the clothing—some lacy lingerie and a few white sweaters—and put them on top of the dryer. I then put my clothes in the washer and started to walk away.

Suddenly I was struck by an idea. I could do a very loving, sensitive thing for my wife. And loving, sensitive things, I told myself, are rare.

I put Norma's delicate items in the dryer to fluff them for five minutes. I had seen her do this before and knew it was what she would have done. After five minutes I would take

Oneness
IS THE
STRENGTH
OF MARRIAGE,
A SAFE
HARBOR

them out of the dryer and hang them in the laundry room.
I could picture her coming downstairs and thanking me,
telling me what a loving, thoughtful husband I was.

So I did that very thing.

I put all her clothes in the dryer and left the laundry room
to do something else. Something that would take five minutes.

But one minute led to three, and suddenly my ADHD
(attention deficit hyperactivity disorder) kicked in and I got
distracted. I had things to do in the kitchen and upstairs and
outside.

About two hours later I went downstairs to the laundry
room. As I stood in front of the washer and dryer, I knew I
was there for some special reason. But I couldn't remember
what it was. I scratched my head, hoping that would help me
remember what I had to do in the laundry room.

Then I remembered.

"Aahhhh, the dryer!" I shouted.

It was worse than I had expected. All of Norma's clothing was totally destroyed. The lace had unraveled and wrapped around other things. The sweaters had shrunk down to the size of Barbie doll clothes.

Suddenly the picture I had of Norma's seeing what I had done was very different from the picture I had two hours earlier, back when putting her clothes in the dryer was a loving, sensitive thing for me to do.

I was in water so hot I could almost feel *myself* unraveling and shrinking.

Then I had another idea.

I know, I thought, *I'll just put these clothes back in the washer, run them through the wash cycle again, and wait for Norma to find them. She'll see them and say to me, "Honey, something's wrong with the washer. I think we need a new one."*

And I, of course, would say, "Yes, dear! I'm sure we do. Let's go get one today!"

Then I'd be out of trouble.

But since honesty and honor go hand in hand and I truly had intended to honor my wife, I let go of the thought almost as quickly as it came to me. *No*, I decided, *I'm going to face this and be honest with her.* I blinked a few times and tried to imagine how I might break the news.

Humor!

Yes, humor always defuses anger. Not only that, but it makes our negotiation process easier. I puzzled for a while about how to make the situation sound funny and then went back upstairs to find Norma. With the courage of an elephant in a field of mice, I opened her office door and tiptoed in.

"Hi, honey," I said, smiling in a way that was meant to test her mood. She looked up from her paperwork and cast me a level gaze.

Then she smiled in a way that said, *Why are you in my office?* Instead she said, "Hi."

I swallowed. "I've got good news and bad news. Which do you want first?" I figured she'd want the bad news since her perfectionistic personality usually wants to get past the negatives.

"What?" She sighed. "I don't understand, but give me the bad news first."

The words began to tumble out. "I want to apologize ahead of time and tell you that I'm really sorry and that I wanted to do a really nice thing for you and that I never meant for it to sour . . . but I dried your clothes."

With a quick gasp, she threw up her hands and started running toward the door. But before she could leave her desk, I gently grabbed her arm. "No, wait, you have to hear the good news."

She looked me right in the eye, and her lips formed a stiff line. "What could possibly be good about this?"

"Well," I said, forcing the corners of my mouth up, "Taylor [our granddaughter] has a brand-new wardrobe!"

That's funny! Don't you think so?

Norma didn't.

She never even cracked a smile. She was out of my grasp instantly, heading downstairs, muttering. When she finally came back up, it was with all the enthusiasm of someone who had just had her purse stolen.

"You've ruined all my lingerie and sweaters! Everything! It's gone. Just like that."

I didn't say anything because the Bible says that even a fool will stay out of trouble if he keeps his mouth shut. I left her alone, and about two hours later, I called her cell phone.

She listened to my apology. Eventually she forgave me. I could feel her spirit opening up to me.

"Hey," I offered. "Want me to take you to the outlet mall in Branson and replace the items?"

She was silent for a while, and I wondered if she had heard me. Finally she spoke: "You just don't understand, do you? Those things are very, very hard to find."

I didn't discuss it anymore. She has all new stuff now, and everything is fine. But the incident points out how easily conflict can arise—especially between two people who are as different as Norma and I are. Norma is very detail-oriented, and she likes to do things by the book. (It obviously works when it comes to drying clothes.) I, on the other hand, am spontaneous and scattered. (That doesn't always work.) Our individual personalities are often vastly different in areas that go beyond the care of delicate clothing.

But along the journey of marriage we have learned how to blend our differences and seek solutions that fan the flame of love that unites us.

Picture it. Our marriage is like the unity-candle display: three candles—two short ones on the outside representing Norma and me as individuals, and a taller one in the center representing our marriage.

Let's take a closer look at the unity candle and the lessons we can learn by studying the flame of oneness.

The Ceremony

If you haven't seen the unity-candle ceremony performed in a wedding, here's how it works. Three candles are placed at the front of the church. At a time early in the ceremony, someone lights the outside candles, leaving the one in the middle unlit. The two lit candles represent the bride and

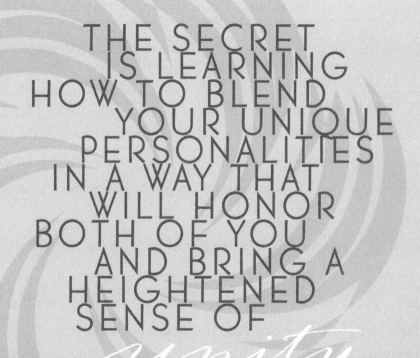

THE SECRET
IS LEARNING
HOW TO BLEND
YOUR UNIQUE
PERSONALITIES
IN A WAY THAT
WILL HONOR
BOTH OF YOU
AND BRING A
HEIGHTENED
SENSE OF
unity

groom before the wedding; they are two individuals. They walk into the church separately; they are still single.

The moment the bride and groom say their vows before God, they're not single anymore. They're married people. They're united.

The two are one.

After the vows have been said, the husband and wife approach the three candles. They take the individual candles, and using those two separate flames, they light the center candle.

The symbolism is beautiful and obvious. No longer will their lights burn for themselves alone. No longer will they live as two single people. Instead, they will enjoy one brighter light, a light that represents the oneness of marriage.

When the Bible speaks of the marriage relationship, it says that when a husband and wife join together, they become "one flesh"; they are united into one (see Genesis 2:24 and Matthew 19:5-6, NIV). The two become bonded together, woven together, blended together.

I believe the beginning of understanding in marriage comes from remembering this: When a husband and wife leave the church, they're not single and separate anymore. If they continue to function as separate people, their marriage will be doomed. The secret is learning how to *blend* the two in a way that will honor both partners and bring a heightened sense of unity.

The two single flames have become one.

The husband and wife have become one.

CHAPTER **2**

*The color
of oneness*

I WANT TO EXPAND this concept of the unity candle for you because I believe that if you understand what the unity-candle display means, will be the basis for marital satisfaction and long-lasting love.

Let me use another image that may help you understand the importance of oneness, the blending that must go on if two single people are to be united.

As I said in the last chapter, when the bride and groom come into the church before the wedding, they are separate people. Picture the groom with his distinct personality, his uniqueness as a male, the issues and influence from his family of origin, his goals and dreams. Then assign a color to that unique blend of factors, let's say the color blue.

Next, picture the bride: she has her own distinct personality, her uniqueness as a female, her own issues and influence from her family of origin, her own goals and dreams—and these may be very different from those of her groom. Assign a very different color to her, perhaps yellow.

Now go back to the unity candle. If the groom is represented by a blue candle and the bride is represented by a yellow candle, what color would their unity candle—their oneness—be? You are right. It would be green. When these two people come together to become one, they blend their differences and "make the color" green. They take their separate lives (blue and yellow) and weave them together in a very special way to become one (green). The more they blend and weave their differences together, the more intimacy and love they will feel.

For many couples, their unity grows in the weeks and months following the wedding. The flame of their oneness burns brightly.

In weddings I've been a part of, I encourage the couple to blow out the flames of the individual candles after they have lit the center candle, representing their desire to place the flame of their oneness above their individual flames.

Oneness Does Not Mean Sameness

The trouble is, becoming one does not mean both people have suddenly become exactly the same. In fact, as soon as they are on their honeymoon, they will probably discover some of their differences. They will discover the "blueness" of the husband and the "yellowness" of the wife.

And here's where many couples get tripped up. When they face those differences and when those differences lead to conflict, the couples revert to their "single"-mindedness, to their own blue and yellow. And when that happens, the flame of oneness flickers.

Here is the best marriage secret I've learned in thirty years: oneness in marriage is maintained not in the *absence of arguments and conflict* but in the *way couples learn how to argue.* Respected marriage experts Howard Markman, Scott Stanley, and Susan Blumberg have found that what keeps couples happily married for a lifetime is not how much they love each other or how much they are committed. What keeps them happily married is how they handle arguments and how they blend as a team throughout their married life. And

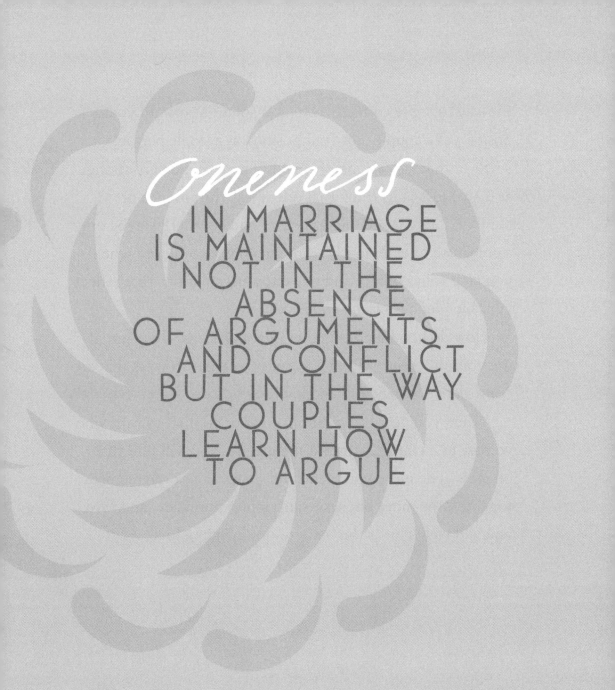

Oneness
IN MARRIAGE
IS MAINTAINED
NOT IN THE
ABSENCE
OF ARGUMENTS
AND CONFLICT
BUT IN THE WAY
COUPLES
LEARN HOW
TO ARGUE

the way to argue correctly is to gear solutions toward your position as a couple, not your position as a single person.

Read that last paragraph again. It may sound very strange at first. Most of us think that oneness is the absence of conflict. But what couple has never had conflict? Maybe only a comatose one. Seriously, though, unity is achieved when you face your conflict and move toward solutions that reflect your blendedness as a couple.

How do you blend together into a oneness? By negotiating your differences and by learning to argue in ways that are constructive, respectful, and loving.

When you gear the solutions to your conflict toward who you are as a couple—toward the green—you will find that oneness. The more you blend and weave your disagreements together, the more oneness, satisfaction, intimacy, and love you will feel. This is the secret to long-lasting love.

WHAT KEEPS
THEM
happily
married
IS HOW THEY
HANDLE ARGUMENTS
AND HOW
THEY BLEND
AS A TEAM
THROUGHOUT
THEIR
MARRIED
LIFE

Your unity candle will dim if one or both of you try to remain single by insisting that your perspective or opinion—your blue or yellow—is right or superior to your spouse's. If each one of you thinks that you are right in your separate opinions, expectations, and concerns, then the war is on and your unity candle will dim.

It's very normal for each of us to think that we are right in most areas, whether we are single or married. But in marriage, our spouse's opinions and concerns are just as important as our own—different but important. And if we wish to experience oneness, to be woven together into a loving couple, we must blend our differences into solutions that represent us. Who we are as a married couple is more important than who we are as individuals. Two are stronger than one.

This ability to gear your solutions to your oneness is so

important that I will devote a whole chapter to helping you learn how you can handle your differences effectively.

But what happens when our differences are allowed free rein? When we no longer consider the importance of the one flame of marital love? The truth is that sometimes the fire of our unity candle grows dim, and other times it is snuffed out completely by divorce.

So how are you doing? I ask again the question I asked at the beginning of this book: Is your flame of oneness still burning brightly?

If not, maybe a destructive wind has made the flame flicker. I have identified five winds that can threaten the marriage flame. If you sense that your flame is flickering, understanding the nature of those five winds can help you protect your marriage from their destructive force.

The good news is that no matter what your unity-candle flame looks like today—if it's barely burning or merely a smoldering wick—it can burn brightly again.

It can even be relit.

CHAPTER 3

Five destructive winds that blow out the unity candle

NONE OF US likes conflict. We know it can damage our relationships, often causing great hurt.

Yet conflict is inevitable in any marriage. Norma and I know that. You do too.

How can we face the differences and friction without allowing them to destroy us? Let's look at five destructive winds that threaten to blow out the flame of oneness in marriage. I developed the idea of these winds from the research of Howard Markman, Scott Stanley, and Susan Blumberg. In their book *Fighting for Your Marriage*, the authors define four risk factors for divorce. I've expanded on those to create the five destructive winds.

There is the *north wind*, which escalates and can leave a crippling storm in its path; the *south wind*, which is warm and seems soothing but leaves behind emptiness and a barren landscape; the *west wind*, which routinely brings in storms and is capable of becoming a tornado; the *east wind*, which will rarely cause immediate damage but which is irritating and constantly blows in dirt; and the *nor'easter*, which takes us by surprise and leaves devastation in its wake.

Remember, even when the flame of the unity candle dances brightly, it can easily be dimmed. And when a couple isn't careful, the flame can be blown out. Notice something very powerful: These destructive winds blow the hardest when one marriage partner relights his or her single candle. People who try to remain more single than married find that their flame of unity will become dim.

In the next few pages I'll tell you about five couples who allowed these destructive winds to seriously dampen or blow out the flame of their unity candles. They are sad stories, situations that led to the weakening of these couples' marriages. But after each story we will take a look at how a couple can calm the storm and protect the unity flame.

As you read these stories, keep in mind the color imagery of the previous chapter and its significance. The husbands and wives have trouble with the winds because they try to take a *single* position to defend their own way instead of trying to find a *oneness* solution. They are more concerned about being blue or yellow instead of working toward a green solution.

As I will explain more fully in the next chapter, how we resolve our arguments is very important. For now, take a look at the five winds, and see if you see yourself in these stories. If you do, make a commitment to calm the storm that presently rages; then avoid the storm in the future by learning how to resolve conflict with the goal of oneness.

North Wind: Escalating Arguments

The north wind builds and builds. It escalates into a fierce storm and can leave a crippling storm in its path. John and Shelly got hit by the north wind.

Cause: Escalating in an Argument. John comes home from work tired and weary from a day of fixing car engines. He trudges into the house and sees his wife, Shelly, in the kitchen. Without taking off his shoes or washing his hands, he comes to her and attempts to kiss her hello.

She squirms away. "Honey, you're a mess. Clean up and then kiss me."

An icy wind blows across John's heart, and he stiffens in response. "You're about as affectionate as an icicle, you know that? Would it kill you to kiss me when I come home?"

The wind touches Shelly, and she drops the spoon in the spaghetti sauce in disgust. "Listen, I work on this house all day. The last thing I need is your grimy fingerprints all over the place." She scowls hard at him. "And maybe I would be a little more affectionate if you didn't stink like a garage."

The north wind blows harder. "Fine. Great. I put in ten hours of hard labor, and this is all the thanks I get!"

"Okay, now don't get me started on thanks." Dinner is

forgotten. Shelly juts out a hip and raises her voice. "You're the most ungrateful person I know! I slave around the house all day and get no thanks at all. At least you get a paycheck."

"Until you spend it on a bunch of junk!" John shouts at her.

Shelly stares at him for a minute and then lets loose the greatest northern gale of all: "Oh, forget it! Why did you bother to come home in the first place?" And with that she storms out of the room.

Can you hear the snuffing sound? That's their unity candle nearly going out.

Remember that before the argument, Shelly was cooking dinner for John, and John wanted nothing more than a kiss. Instead, neither John nor Shelly will have the appetite to eat dinner that night, and both will go to sleep feeling angry and sick. It will be three days before the ice melts enough so they

talk to each other again. This is a sad picture of the predict-
able effects of an escalating argument and the damage possible when the north wind blows out a couple's flame of
oneness.

Escalation in an argument happens when two married
people revert to defending their individual needs and agenda.
When they don't consider their needs as a couple or the
unity they need to protect, their flame is in danger of being
extinguished. They forget that the flame burns brightest
when their individual needs and agenda are blended.

Calm the Wind: Avoid Escalation. Arguments escalate when a
husband or wife concludes that the other person has a differing point of view but believes that point of view is stupid and
unnecessary. An argument will escalate in our home if I tell
Norma that her perfectionism is wrong and that my flexibility

is right. Likewise, the north wind blows if I tell her to loosen up, saying things like, "You're just being ridiculous."

Do you see the "single" colors coming out? Neither John nor Shelly is thinking about a green solution. They are too tied up in their own selfish agendas.

Escalation occurs when blue or yellow is more important than green. Instead of thinking of what's best for them as a couple, they get stuck on what's best for them as individuals. They become afraid that they might miss out on something they personally want or that their desires and expectations might not be met.

Look at John and Shelly's behavior. Instead of ignoring his wife's comment about cleaning up, John snaps back with a comment of his own. Both are acting out of a desire to please themselves, to be self-satisfied, instead of acting out of a desire to do what's best for them as a couple. John gets stuck thinking about what's best for him. He finds it distasteful to think that he might be denied something he wants or that his needs might be ignored.

As spouses' anger at not getting their way increases, a chain reaction of consequences begins to take place. If that reaction continues, the couple could be heading down the treacherous path toward divorce, which would blow out the unity candle forever.

That's the simple but powerful truth.

This type of escalation in arguing is basic to our self-centered human nature. However, real harmony in marriage comes from remembering that when we marry, we are not single anymore. Blue and yellow have to become green. We must understand that marriage includes the ability to lay our own desires on the table. We must learn to trust that our spouse will handle who we are in a way that is caring and honoring. We must agree to extend this same type of care and honor to our spouse regarding his or her desires too.

If you are to avoid escalation during a disagreement, you must seek to resolve issues from a *couple* perspective. Remember this: When you win as a couple, you and your spouse will both be happier as individuals as well.

In summary, remember these key points in order to avoid escalation during an argument:

- Leave your "single"-minded pride at the altar. It is impossible to find solutions that favor oneness when pride is in the way.
- Learn how to communicate better. (Suggestions are included in the following chapters.)
- If you find yourself or your spouse escalating an argument, draw back and give each other time and space. When emotions have cooled, try again to establish the goal in love: oneness.

WHEN
YOU
WIN
AS A
couple
YOU AND
YOUR SPOUSE
WILL BOTH
BE HAPPIER
AS INDIVIDUALS
AS WELL

South Wind: Avoidance and Withdrawal

The south wind is warm and seems soothing, but it can leave behind emptiness and a barren landscape. Joe and Lana got hit by the south wind.

Cause: Avoiding an Argument or Withdrawing. One evening as Lana is sorting through the bills and balancing the checkbook, she notices a problem. According to the checkbook, Joe didn't stop and put gas in the car. She looks up and sees him across the family room, watching college basketball on television. Lana calls to him, "Honey, did you stop for gas as I asked?"

Joe is deeply engrossed in the game and hears the question only after Lana has asked it twice. "Uh . . ." He lets his voice trail off. It's a playoff game late in the fourth quarter, and he's far more interested in the score than her question. "Yeah, I think I forgot."

Lana stares at him and sighs. Is it fair that she works on the bills while he watches a game? "You know, Joe, it really bugs me when . . ."

It's a commercial break, so Joe gives her his full attention. "What? What bugs you?"

The soothing south wind begins to blow. *Why fight with him?* Lana figures. She can always fill the tank tomorrow. "Never mind."

Joe looks at her strangely. "I hate it when you tell me never mind. If you have something to say, say it."

Suddenly everything about Joe's attitude is more than Lana can stand. But the last thing she wants is a confrontation, so she collects the bills, stands up, and glares at Joe. "Forget it. You wouldn't understand anyway."

By the time Lana gets upstairs, her blood is boiling, and she can easily think of a dozen things she would like to tell Joe,

none of them pleasant. Meanwhile, he's downstairs hating the
way she constantly huffs off by herself.

The warm south wind creates barren places, and not just in
Joe and Lana's love life. Avoiding an argument or withdrawing will eventually cause them both a lot of stress as
well.

All Lana wanted to do was avoid fighting with her
husband. But in the process, the seductive south wind blew
the flame of their unity candle down to almost nothing.

This is the way the south wind works. You might think
avoiding arguments is a way of saving your relationship or
making it run more smoothly. Instead, you are creating a
lifeless marriage that can easily result in a house with
two strangers living together. Very often this leads to
divorce.

As long as Lana withdraws and keeps her color to herself,

she and Joe will not find a green solution. Green isn't green without yellow.

If you close off your spouse, you're reacting like a single person again, saying, "I don't want to talk about this. It's too dangerous to talk to you. It upsets me too much, so I refuse to do this." That, in turns, sends an even worse message: "The person I am on the inside is private to me, and I'm not going to share it with you, so we're stuck. You can't become one with me because I won't let you."

Besides the obvious lack of communication, this behavior and mind-set cause deep anger in both spouses. If you have this type of anger, distrust, and isolation in your marriage, then your flame of oneness is dimming even as I write this.

Calm the Wind: Communicate. Norma and I know how important it is to keep very short anger lists in our hearts. Therefore, we decide to talk and open up in an honoring way even when we may not feel like it. We try to take charge of our emotions and not let them control us.

Sometimes the word *stress* is used as a socially acceptable word for *anger*. When we look at anger closely, we find that it is caused by one of three triggers: fear, frustration, or hurt feelings.

Lana's anger was rooted in her frustration about Joe's forgetfulness and then his unwillingness to talk with her about the problem. She also was afraid of what might happen if she pressed the issue with Joe. So she shut down.

Think of what the situation might have looked like if she and Joe had pursued open communication about her frustration. Lana could have explained her frustration to Joe when he tried to talk with her during a commercial. Joe could have acknowledged that he had not followed through on getting gas and could have promised to hear Lana's frustration—

Open communication BEGINS BY MAKING A COMMITMENT NEVER TO BURY THE ISSUES

maybe not at that moment because the game was nearly over, but he could have said, "Lana, I'm so sorry I forgot. I sense that you are frustrated. Can we talk about it in a few minutes after the game is over?"

Open communication begins by making a commitment never to bury the issues. You cannot have a brightly burning flame of oneness if you are hiding emotions, feelings, and circumstances from the other person. You cannot be green without both blue and yellow.

At the same time, if you are letting outside distractions deter you from truly listening to your spouse, it may be time to check your priorities. No television program is worth making your spouse bury his or her feelings, especially when unresolved anger is such a destructive wind in marriage.

West Wind: False or Unrealistic Beliefs

The west wind brings in storms and is capable of becoming a tornado. Denny and Kate got hit by a west wind.

Cause: False Beliefs or Exaggerated Negative Beliefs about Your Spouse.
Denny trudges across the living-room floor with a bag of garbage in each hand. Across the room, Kate sits in a corner chair, chatting with her mother on a long-distance telephone call. Her feet are propped up, and she is taking part in a happy, animated conversation.

"Could you at least open the door?" Denny asks Kate. He hates the hours Kate spends on the phone. He waits while Kate crosses the room and does as he asked.

When he finishes the task, he returns and stares at his wife. *She's so lazy,* he thinks to himself. *Every weekend she sits around while I do all the work.*

The longer he stands watching her, the more disgusted he becomes. *She's too attached to her mother. She doesn't care about my needs at all. Look at her, lounging when she could be helping me. Back when we first got married she was fun and pretty and didn't talk on the phone so much and . . .*

By the time Kate gets off the phone, Denny is so frustrated with her that they have a terrible evening together, maybe even a yelling match or two. The west wind has taken its toll. It has worked its way into Denny's mind and caused him to view everything about his wife through storm-clouded eyes. The resulting storm is a serious threat to the flame of their unity candle.

Calm the Wind: Check Your Vision. If you see more negative than positive things in your spouse, you're not looking clearly and your relationship is starting to go downhill. If you cannot recognize or appreciate your spouse's qualities—his or her color—you will never truly become one.

Marriage expert John Gottman of the University of Washington in Seattle says that you need a ratio of five positives to one negative in order to have a healthy, long-lasting marriage.

If this is a problem for you, here's your assignment: take some time alone to write a list of every positive thing you can identify about your spouse. Here are some examples of traits that may be overlooked: faithful, honest, hardworking, consistent, funny, serious, loyal, dependable, friendly, helpful, and talented.

The list goes on. Look for the positives even if it takes awhile to come up with a list. If this is a struggle for you, you're probably out of practice, so give yourself time. The positive traits are there if you look hard enough.

I have discovered that to be the case with thousands of couples who had succumbed to the life-sucking temptation of negativity. Once husbands and wives are trained to see their spouses in a positive light, their marriages almost always improve. This has certainly been true for Norma and me. For a long time I thought Norma's perfectionism was ruining us! I didn't take the time to see anything positive about that part of her. I had to make a conscious effort to find positive things to think about instead.

Obviously, today I think many more positive things than negative things about who she is. That's how we live our lives. Maybe someday we'll both have such positive admiration for each other that we'll never have another negative thought. It might be possible. We're working toward that end, and by doing that, we're avoiding the stormy winds from the west.

East Wind: Belittling or Invalidating

The east wind will rarely cause immediate damage, but it is

irritating and constantly blows in dirt. Beth and Ben got hit by the east wind.

Cause: Belittling or Invalidating Your Spouse. Beth is getting dressed for bed when she hears her husband, Ben, helping their son in the next room. The boy has been sick for the past two days, so Beth makes her way to the room. "What's happening?" Beth demands. Ben is rocking their son, Jimmy, but the child is coughing quite hard.

Ben puts a finger to his lips and looks at Beth. "It's okay, I have it under control. He's almost back to sleep."

Crossing the room, Beth takes the child from her husband and rolls her eyes at the same time. "He needs cough syrup. Anyone can see that."

Ben isn't sure how to react as Beth scoops their son into her arms. "I would have given it to him if his cough got worse."

Beth stops in the doorway and cocks her head in a way that makes Ben feel like a dim-witted child. "If you know so much about kids, how come you forgot to put an ice pack in Sara's lunch today? You made her a meat sandwich, remember?" She pauses but not long enough for Ben to answer. "Meat sandwiches need an ice pack, or the kids will get sick."

Insecurity sets in, and it's the direct result of a wind from the east. Nothing strong, nothing that will cause Ben and Beth to yell and spew mean things at each other. But this incessant, nagging wind will circle around a mountain of issues and blow in dirt from all sides. It's the type of wind that sets people's teeth on edge without ever being obvious. Ben stands, scratches his forehead, and makes a last-ditch attempt. "I'll help."

Beth stifles a chuckle. "No, that's okay. You would just be in the way. Go to bed, and I'll be there in a few minutes."

When Ben turns in for the night, he isn't sure what just happened. He and Beth didn't really have a fight, but his stomach is churning all the same. When he had been alone with his son, his thoughts had been on the wonders of parenthood and the hope of sharing intimacy with his wife later that evening. Now, though, he has lost interest completely.

Without realizing it, Beth is allowing the east wind to have its way with their marriage. Day by day the grit will build until finally it's too late to do anything about it, and suddenly this couple will wonder what happened to the flame of their unity candle.

Belittling your spouse works like this: you begin to think that your needs are superior to your spouse's in one or more areas. Buying into this lie, allowing this wind to have its way, is one of the most destructive dynamics in marriage today. Disapproval or superiority can be expressed with facial expressions, tone of voice, and body language as loudly as if you were saying, "Sweetheart, I love you, but in this area, you're inferior to me." You send a clear message: your opinions, experiences, and concerns are better than those of your spouse.

If you insist that blue is better than yellow—or vice versa—your marriage is doomed. Green isn't green if you try to remove or obliterate the blue or yellow from the blend. Value both colors as necessary parts of the green.

The truth of the matter is that your spouse is a very valuable person to God and others. When you belittle him or her, you are belittling one of God's creations, the person you loved enough to marry. Your criticisms and faultfinding only diminish your spouse and are like the sand and grit that blow in with the east wind, endangering the strength of the flame of your unity candle.

Calm the Wind: Speak Uplifting Words. Another truth is that your spouse is a person of unique strengths and weaknesses. You may not appreciate your spouse's value because you have not taken the time to think about his or her positive qualities. Search for them as you would search for a priceless treasure.

But it is not enough to *think about* your spouse's positive qualities; you must also learn to *say them aloud.* Instead of letting the east wind tempt you to use your tongue to belittle or invalidate your spouse, discipline yourself to speak praise about him or her.

Let's look at Beth's situation. Even if she felt as if she could do a better job of caring for their son, she could have said to her husband, "Ben, you are such a tender father. You have been a real comfort to Jimmy. Thanks for giving me some relief. Even though you've nearly gotten him to sleep, I think he needs a little more cough syrup before he nods off. Shall I take him?"

Beth's words would have protected Ben's self-esteem, helped Jimmy think of his father as a valuable person, and even helped her see Ben's contribution to their family. Words that build up a spouse also build up a marriage. These benefits are so good they cannot be compared with anything else. Several marriage experts report that rehearsing your spouse's positive assets is the best action you can take to build a strong, healthy marriage.

The key here is that in order to maintain your unity, both of you must listen to and value the other. Watch your partner more closely, and notice things he or she does well. Remember this ratio: think five positive thoughts about your spouse for every negative one. Then apply your new thoughts to your interaction with your spouse. This will help you avoid belittling and in turn will build self-esteem in your partner and confidence in your relationship. Both of these strengths will lead to a closer intimacy with God as well.

IT IS
NOT ENOUGH
TO THINK ABOUT
YOUR SPOUSE'S
*positive
qualities*
YOU MUST ALSO
LEARN TO SAY THEM
ALOUD

When you speak affirming, life-giving words, you are intentionally sheltering the flame of your unity candle from the dirt of the east wind.

Nor'easter:
Withholding Information or Dropping a Bomb

The nor'easter—the rare northeastern wind that blows off the ocean and pounds the East Coast with storms—takes us by surprise and leaves devastation in its wake. Suzanne and Tom got hit by a nor'easter.

Cause: Withholding Information, Lying, or Dropping a Bomb. Suzanne was sitting at the breakfast table when Tom walked up to her, tossed the morning paper on the table, and said, "I haven't loved you in two years."

Never, not once in their marriage, had Suzanne seen that

The Key

HERE IS
THAT IN ORDER
TO MAINTAIN
YOUR UNITY
BOTH OF YOU
MUST LISTEN TO
AND VALUE
THE OTHER

comment coming. She and Tom had two small children and seemed to be living the American dream.

Until that morning.

Almost overnight Tom moved into an apartment across town. Left with no way of supporting herself and the kids, Suzanne had to find a job and move the children into a small rental unit. The whole time Suzanne felt as if she were caught in a hurricane. How could Tom have waited two years to tell her? Didn't he love her enough to share his feelings with her back when they still could have worked on their relationship? Suzanne began using alcohol to numb her pain, and twice she tried to kill herself. In less than a month she was suffering from the physical symptoms of depression.

This is exactly the type of thing that can happen when a couple experiences the devastating effects of a nor'easter. Not only is the flame of the unity candle snuffed out immediately with such a pronouncement, but the spouse taken by surprise is literally destroyed—emotionally and physically—in the process.

The nor'easter is the prevailing wind when one of the marriage partners has an affair or emotionally checks out of a marriage for months and years at a time. It brings the bombshell announcement that often leads to an immediate separation or divorce.

The storm doesn't always start with a bombshell. It may come after a history of keeping crucial information from a spouse or when the marriage becomes littered with lies. A married woman begins having business lunches with a single man she finds stimulating and attractive. At first she merely omits the details of her lunch when she and her husband talk at the end of the day.

But as her time with her single colleague becomes more

important to her, she will almost always lie to allow herself the ability to continue having her way. Eventually she will feel as if her husband doesn't know her, and the sad thing is she'll be right.

When that happens, the bombshell announcement is not far away.

Calm the Wind: Learn How to Argue. In a sense, avoiding this wind is as basic as avoiding the other four winds combined. Do not allow your arguments to escalate, do not give in to the temptation to avoid discussions when issues come up, do not think negatively about your spouse, and do not belittle him or her.

That may sound simple, but if you are caught in the midst of a nor'easter, you must hold on to one of the calming forces above and dig as deeply into that area as possible. If you find

DECIDE NOW
NEVER TO LIE
TO YOUR SPOUSE
HE OR SHE IS
YOUR OTHER
HALF

Truth

WILL KEEP YOU
BONDED
TOGETHER

yourself intentionally withholding information or even lying to your spouse, it's time to come clean. Make a commitment to tell your spouse everything that's even remotely questionable. This will help keep your actions illuminated by the light of the flame of oneness. Decide now never to lie to your spouse. He or she is your other half. Truth will keep you bonded together.

Don't forget: the goal is to keep the unity candle burning brightly and to keep the focus on being a couple.

Avoiding the five destructive winds is only one way to keep the candle of oneness burning in your marriage. In the next chapter I'll tell you another crucial detail that will keep the fire alive: learning how to argue in light of your oneness.

CHAPTER **4**

Learning to fight right

CONFLICTS ARE INEVITABLE in a relationship in which two people—with different temperaments, different personalities, different styles, different backgrounds, different skills, different strengths, and different weaknesses—come together as one.

Differences are not a bad thing—not at all.

Blue and yellow are wonderful colors, great colors. Achieving oneness does not mean that blue and yellow cease to exist. No, each is a vital part of yet another wonderful color: green.

The problem with differences, though, is that many husbands and wives don't know how to handle them well. In their attempt to resolve their stresses, they often begin to argue and feel separate again. The flame of their unity candle, their oneness, is threatened.

Remember, it's important to learn how to argue in a marriage if your relationship with your spouse is to be strong and fulfilling. When two people toss all that they are on the table and attempt to make harmony of it, disagreements are bound to happen. And that is okay. Disagreements can be wonderfully constructive. Here's the catch: in the midst of a disagreement, the two people must examine their differing personality traits and opinions and find a way to negotiate a solution that benefits them as a couple and a team.

As we have been discussing, when blue and yellow disagree, the trick is to come up with a green solution. This new green solution is stronger than either individual, single solution!

This is the truth: The only time you have to worry about a divorce is when one of you starts becoming "single" again—either in mind-set or in actions. When one person starts believing that the solution has to represent his or her way of thinking, trouble is brewing. Big trouble.

So how do a blue-thinking person and a yellow-thinking person come to a green solution? Let's look at some suggestions for how "single"-minded people can achieve a couple focus.

How to Fight Right. Research I've done over the past two decades has taught me that the way a married couple can disagree correctly is to do so *in light of their oneness*. These are the key steps in learning how to fight right:

1. *Love, love, love.* The first step is love, unconditional love that will not be threatened by a disagreement. With this never-say-die, divorce-is-not-an-option type of love, you will be free to disagree in peace and look together for the right answer.

2. *Reveal your positions.* The next step is to explain your point of view to one another. As you do, remember that the sum is greater than the parts. In other words, the couple you make together is more important than your individual desires, needs, thoughts, and opinions. In your marriage, green is stronger than either blue or yellow alone.

3. *Communicate freely.* Conversation and discussion about your differences are good. Explain completely your needs and your feelings about an issue. Then allow your spouse the same privilege.

4. *Remain matter-of-fact.* Keep emotions out of the discussion. Disagreeing is an act, not an attack. Don't feel person-

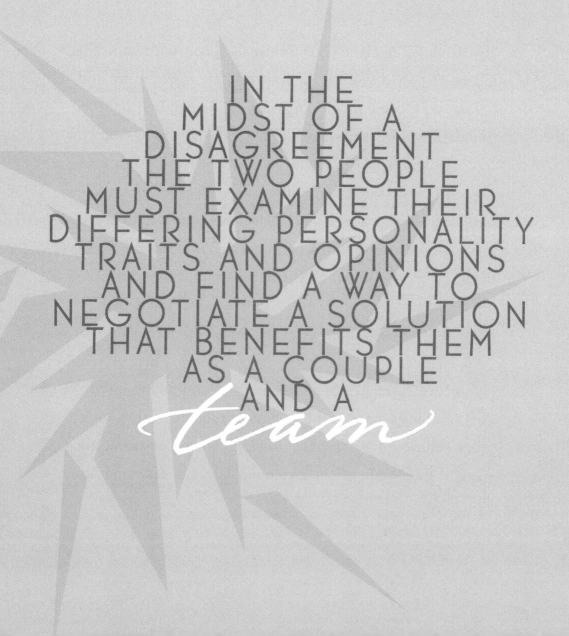

IN THE
MIDST OF A
DISAGREEMENT
THE TWO PEOPLE
MUST EXAMINE THEIR
DIFFERING PERSONALITY
TRAITS AND OPINIONS
AND FIND A WAY TO
NEGOTIATE A SOLUTION
THAT BENEFITS THEM
AS A COUPLE
AND A
team

ally damaged because your spouse disagrees with you. This means you need to keep the tone of your voices warm and loving, your eye contact nonaccusing. Remember that the foundation you stand on is one of God-given love.

5. *Analyze the different positions you each take, and discuss them as a couple.* At this stage, it's important to work as long as it takes until both of you understand the other's position. In my marriage, this is the step when I need to understand Norma's detail-oriented nature and she needs to understand my flexible nature. It's a meeting of the minds and a time when compassion ought to be expressed between partners.

6. *Decide on the best decision for you as a couple.* This will require laying aside your personal individuality and taking on the goal of doing what's best to maintain oneness. Work for a green solution. It's important to reach an agreement at this stage of the discussion. If it's slow in coming, take time to

pray together as a couple. In my experience, the solution will seem that much clearer.

7. *Agree not to be angry or emotional.* If you work toward a solution, but it's not really the one you want, don't allow yourself to fret or stew about it. Remember that the goal is to find a solution that works for you *as a couple,* not one that best addresses *only your* wants or needs.

8. *Don't look back.* Don't keep score. And don't feel as if either of you lost or won. Rather remind yourselves that you will both win every time as long as disagreements are worked out in light of your oneness.

A Lesson from Ephesians

Unity and oneness come at a cost: self-sacrifice. And for most of us it's hard to give up our positions and opinions.

However, the Bible is clear that when we submit to each

other—with all our differences—we must do so out of reverence for Christ. When we allow for the other's point of view, for his or her experience and expertise, we must do so out of reverence for Christ. When we take into account the other's weaknesses, we must not do so to take advantage of the other's weakness but to make up for the weakness with our strength—all out of reverence for Christ.

Let's look at what the Bible says about selfless love in Ephesians 5:21-33. In some ways these verses read like a short list on how to love your spouse. It is also a good strategy for keeping the flame of oneness alive and burning brightly in your marriage. Every verse shouts about selfless love. Let this passage give you direction about how to love your husband or wife.

> *Submit to one another out of reverence for Christ. You wives will submit to your husbands as you do to the Lord. For a husband is the head of his wife as Christ is the head of his body, the church; he gave*

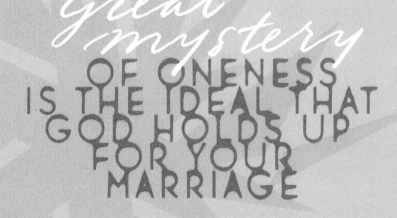

The
great
mystery
OF ONENESS
IS THE IDEAL THAT
GOD HOLDS UP
FOR YOUR
MARRIAGE

his life to be her Savior. As the church submits to Christ, so you wives must submit to your husbands in everything.

And you husbands must love your wives with the same love Christ showed the church. He gave up his life for her to make her holy and clean, washed by baptism and God's word. He did this to present her to himself as a glorious church without a spot or wrinkle or any other blemish. Instead, she will be holy and without fault. In the same way, husbands ought to love their wives as they love their own bodies. For a man is actually loving himself when he loves his wife. No one hates his own body but lovingly cares for it, just as Christ cares for his body, which is the church. And we are his body.

As the Scriptures say, "A man leaves his father and mother and is joined to his wife, and the two are united into one." This is a great mystery, but it is an illustration of the way Christ and the church are one. So again I say, each man must love his wife as he loves himself, and the wife must respect her husband.

The great mystery of oneness is the ideal that God holds up for your marriage. Be inspired by this passage to love your spouse with a self-giving love, a love that seeks not its own way but the good of the marriage.

Learning how to handle conflict well is a key step in maintaining the oneness you've always wanted. But there's even more you can do to fan the flame of unity. Read on to find out how to L-O-V-E in ways that will strengthen your marital oneness.

CHAPTER 5

Learning to L·O·V·E

*A*LL YOU NEED IS LOVE," the Beatles sang in the sixties and seventies. On some level they were right. We all need love. The Beatles may not have had in mind the kind of selfless love described in the Ephesians passage, but they did know that love is essential to relation-ships.

Let me unpack the word *love* in a way that will help you gain some tools for deepening your marriage and ensuring the unity needed for it to endure. I would like you to see L-O-V-E with these four components:

Listen

Offer yourself

Value and honor

Embrace

Let's explore these components one by one to see how they can work in your marriage.

Listen

You cannot have an intimate, satisfying, emotionally healthy relationship unless you communicate. And one of the foundations of communication is listening.

Oneness in marriage is deepened when you listen to your spouse.

What does it mean to listen?

Think about your communication with your spouse. You come to each other with your ideas, your hopes, your frustrations, your fears, and your needs. What happens then? How can you hear one another and attempt to understand, as clearly as you can, your spouse's point of view?

First, let your spouse speak. Your initial goal is to hear what he or she is saying. Make direct eye contact. Do whatever you can to encourage your spouse to express his or her thoughts or feelings. Don't correct your spouse. Don't respond to what you hear. Just let your spouse know that you hear what he or she is saying.

Then transition into understanding. Spend as much time as you need to make sure you understand your spouse's point of view. Ask questions that will help you determine if you have understood your spouse's words. "I want to make sure that I understand you correctly. Is this what you mean?" Then give your spouse a summary of what you heard.

Often after I have summarized what I think Norma has said to me, I will ask her, "Am I clear on this, or have I missed the point?"

She often will say, "No, you've missed the point. Let me explain it differently. Maybe I can use a word picture to help you understand what I'm saying." Then she will try another method to explain her thought or feeling in different words.

A key principle Norma and I keep in mind is this: I'm 100 percent responsible to understand, and she is 100 percent responsible to explain it in a way that I can understand.

It is important not to give up until you find a way to understand each other. Ask as many questions as necessary to help

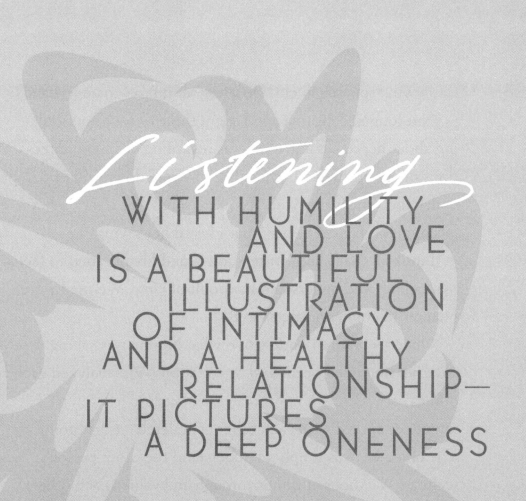

Listening
WITH HUMILITY
AND LOVE
IS A BEAUTIFUL
ILLUSTRATION
OF INTIMACY
AND A HEALTHY
RELATIONSHIP—
IT PICTURES
A DEEP ONENESS

clarify your spouse's intent. Do whatever it takes to understand.

Not long ago Norma and I spent three or four hours talking about her needs and concerns regarding changing directions in our business. As she talked, I wrote down what I understood she was saying. To make sure I was clear on her meaning, I repeated to her what I heard her saying.

I took all that I had written down, and I really tried to feel her feelings and understand her point of view. We used word pictures to communicate as well.

Once I was sure I understood what Norma was saying, I gave her my list of needs and expectations. We analyzed each other's lists. This was nonthreatening because we weren't saying we agreed with each other completely at that point. The objective was simply to understand the other person's feelings. We thought things through and valued each other's opinions.

Next we discussed possible solutions in light of our oneness, our unity. I felt safe to share what I thought and felt, and she felt safe to share what she thought and felt. As I understood her needs and she understood mine, she was thinking of ways to resolve the situation. I was doing the same thing. We tried to find solutions that would make us both feel valued and honored and solutions that would bene-fit us as a couple first and foremost, regardless of which of our individual needs were put aside in the process.

That is a picture of true listening and oneness.

Often your spouse simply wants to know that you are listening and that you understand. Sometimes that in itself can solve the whole thing. That's the amazing thing about open communication. It is so powerful!

It is so powerful because we are vulnerable, connected, and committed. We're in love, and this type of communication increases our love for one another. The truth is, where God's love and mercy grows, pride isn't found. And pride is the source of feeling single in a marriage.

Listening with humility and love is a beautiful illustration of intimacy and a healthy relationship. It pictures a deep oneness. The excitement comes from finding a solution that is higher than your own personal solution.

Offer Yourself

Research has shown that if you offer yourself to your spouse, you are more likely to enjoy a healthy, long-lasting, loving bond. What if you're married to someone who doesn't want to offer himself or herself? The principle still holds. Although it's difficult, try to be less concerned with what the other person in the relationship is doing for you and more concerned with what you are doing for him or her.

COMMIT
YOURSELF
TO SPENDING
TWENTY MINUTES
A DAY
INTENTIONALLY
MEETING
*your
spouse's
needs*

After listening to your spouse's needs, identify several that you will begin to nurture and meet. Maybe that means a conversation when you're too tired to talk or a walk around the block when your feet are tired. It might mean actively listening more or giving the kids a bath before bedtime. Whatever it is, identify your spouse's needs and then work on meeting them wherever possible.

To make that goal measurable, commit yourself to spending twenty minutes a day intentionally meeting your spouse's needs. It will make a huge difference.

If you are uncertain about your spouse's needs or if you are not sure he or she knows what your needs are, set aside an evening when you can take separate pieces of paper and write down endings to these sentence openers: "I feel loved when you . . . " or "What would be very meaningful to me is . . ." Do not limit yourselves. If you can fill up two pieces of paper, do so. This will provide you both with a wealth of information on how to understand and meet each other's needs.

Value and Honor

Giving value and honor to someone is giving distinction to that person, giving worth to him or her. The New Testament reminds us to "be devoted to one another in brotherly love [genuine affection]. Honor one another above yourselves" (Romans 12:10, NIV). Other passages direct us to think of others as better than ourselves (see Philippians 2:3). It's similar to the principle Jesus taught when he asked us to love our neighbors as we love ourselves.

Recognize that your spouse's opinions are very valuable, even if they differ from yours. Value the ways in which he or she is different from you. Then learn to celebrate those differences. Instead of complaining about them, learn to say things such as, "You are incredible. I never would have thought of doing that [or doing it that way or looking at it that way]. I'm getting a clearer picture of who you are."

Sometimes your spouse's opinion will be even more valuable than your own. For instance, with Norma and me, I had to understand that the beauty of our oneness was found in blending her unique personality with my uniqe personality. I had to value her "yellowness." Our marriage has grown tremendously since I've started valuing and honoring her, cherishing her personality traits that are different from mine.

I truly believe this is a difficult thing to do in our own strength. Why? Because our human nature is selfish. We are much more concerned about our own well-being than that of our spouse. Sometimes the last thing we want to do is honor or value our spouse. Without God's help, we might be angry

BY SHIFTING
OUR FOCUS
TO WHAT'S
*good and
right and
excellent*
ABOUT OUR
SPOUSES—
OUR NEGATIVE
THINKING
ACTUALLY
REVERSES
AND WE BEGIN
TO SEE
OUR SPOUSES
DIFFERENTLY

and frustrated and ready to walk out the door—possibly even out of the marriage.

Realize that we all change through the years. It's important to maintain an interest in better understanding your spouse. As your feelings and needs change and as you gain more wisdom through the years, different things may become more important to you. The deeper your relationship with your spouse grows, the safer both of you will feel in sharing the essence of who you are.

Journal of Honor. I have found it very helpful to keep what I call a journal of honor. In it I write down the reasons I value God and the reasons I value Norma. My wife's perfectionism—a quality that caused friction in the early days of our marriage—is now high on the list of assets that I consider priceless.

In my journal of honor, I have more than five pages full of

reasons why my wife is so valuable to me. I keep the list close at hand, and I often tell her why I value her. It is one way I can honor her.

I encourage you to start such a journal. Start by writing about God. Tell him why you value and highly esteem him and love him more than anyone or anything else.

Then move on to the reasons you value and honor your spouse. When you start your list, write down every good thing you can think of. Then add to the list regularly. List the reasons why your spouse is important to you, why his or her uniqueness is valuable.

Write in your journal of honor at least once a month, and set aside time to share the contents with your spouse. For a romantic evening, read some of your list to your spouse. If he or she is making a list about you, your spouse may be willing to share that list with you.

On a regular basis tell your spouse why he or she is so valuable to you. This might mean praising those traits when they come to mind; putting sticky notes in your spouse's purse or wallet; surprising your partner with a list of his or her positive qualities; or telling children and friends why you value your spouse, both in your spouse's presence and behind his or her back. Believe me, when your spouse hears that you've bragged about him or her, it will be a real boost to your partner's self-esteem.

Sadly, our human tendency is to focus on the negative qualities of our spouses: what they lack, how they could look better, how they could love better, or how they aren't meeting our needs.

By shifting our focus to what's good and right and excellent about our spouses, our negative thinking actually reverses, and we begin to see our spouses differently. Watch how that strengthens your relationship and makes you more grateful for each other.

Embrace

Without a doubt, physical touch remains one of the best ways to convey love. I first discussed this in the book *The Blessing*, which John Trent and I wrote several years ago. But I believe the message as strongly today as I did then. Brushes of the finger on your spouse's arms or face, hugs, kisses, and skin-to-skin contact will always be ways to convey a thousand words about love.

Physical touch tells your spouse, "I love you, I need you, I like you. You're worth a lot to me, and I don't want you to go away."

There's nothing like physical touch to make us feel loved, accepted, and desired.

Ten Ways to Add a Touch of Love to Your Marriage. If you are not a person who naturally demonstrates love through physical touch, here are a few ways you can get started:

1. Hug when you leave each other in the morning and when you see each other again in the evening.

2. Work in the kitchen or at some other project together. Be playful, letting your arms brush against each other now and then.

3. Put extra lotion on your hands, and ask to rub the leftover cream onto your spouse's hands.

4. Offer to give your spouse a hand massage, working your fingers into the tendons and muscles of your spouse's entire hand.

5. Sit together when watching television or a movie. If your spouse sits in an easy chair, sit on the floor between his

or her legs. This way you have contact with your spouse's body throughout the show.

6. Offer to give your spouse a massage.

7. Hold hands when you're driving in the car together. Make up a private sign—such as three hand squeezes—to communicate "I love you."

8. Kiss more often. Freshen your breath, soften your lips, and have at it. Remember how much fun you had kissing before you were married? Why stop now?

9. Allow yourself to be intimate in places you haven't thought of before—the clothes closet, the shower, the kitchen. Spontaneous touch is always a good thing.

10. Don't grope without warning. There's nothing more irritating to most women than to be bending over doing something with, say, the dishwasher when you come up and give them a pinch. This is not a good type of touch for most women.

The benefits of physical touch are so tremendous, there's simply no reason to wait. Try these on your spouse today! You may be surprised at how fulfilling an embrace between you and your husband or wife can be.

Using the L-O-V-E Elements in Everyday Life

Norma and I have had many opportunities to put the L-O-V-E elements into practice, not only to handle conflict but also to maintain the oneness that is so important to us.

We recently built a new house. For those of you who have gone through this experience, I may not need to say anything more. You know the conflicts that can arise as you and your spouse face the countless decisions—many more than either of you ever anticipated—that go into building a new house. If a husband and wife can make it through building or remodeling a house, they can make it through almost anything.

Sadly, however, many couples do not survive a project like this because they do not communicate in a way that is honoring. Their relationship is strained. The five destructive winds hit their marriage, and the flame goes out.

Norma and I soon became aware that the house-building project could become a destructive wind for us. We committed ourselves to using the listening, offering ourselves, valuing and honoring, and embracing skills. We were able to listen to the needs, concerns, and opinions each of us had regarding the house. We talked through those issues until we understood each other. Then we offered ourselves to each other and committed ourselves to meeting as many of the other's needs as we could. We valued and honored each other by focusing on the positive rather than the negative aspects of what we were doing together. We embraced each other, remembering to encourage each other and express our love through tender touch.

In doing so, we resolved issues relating to the size of the house, the placement of bathrooms, the exterior wood, the interior design, and many more details. Despite our personal differences, we had very little conflict.

We hope that you can keep the flame of your oneness burning brightly. Through the stressful times. Through the good times. Through a lifetime together.

CHAPTER **6**

*Keep
the flame
burning
forever*

JOE AND MARLENE fell in love in high school and married when they were in their early twenties. Joe spent three years fighting in World War II, during which time Marlene wrote him numerous letters. One of them said this:

My Dearest Joe,

I feel as if I am with you, beside you in battle, and looking over you as evening falls. God quickens my heart when you are in need and puts prayers in my heart when danger comes. The very truth is that when you breathe, my chest rises; when you cry, my eyes grow damp. We are one, my love. Missing you is like missing my arm or my leg or my very heart. I will not be complete until your return . . .

Your loving wife,
Marlene

Joe did return, and the candle of this couple's oneness burned brightly for another five decades. They raised a family and lived to see grandchildren and great-grandchildren.

Did they disagree? Sure. But they understood how to avoid the five destructive winds. They knew how to listen to each other and understand each other. They valued and honored each other as naturally as they breathed.

Just to remember the depth of their love, every now and then they would cuddle up on the sofa and read the letters they had written to each other during those dark days of the war.

And in this way their love continued to burn brightly until one day Joe's heart gave out. With Marlene at his side he moved on to be with the Lord.

Three days later, Marlene stopped breathing in her sleep.

When her adult children found her the next morning, her hands were settled peacefully over her heart, and there was an unforgettable smile on her face.

Not one of their children was surprised by what seemed a tragic string of events.

"You see," their oldest son said. "Mom and Dad were so

closely connected that when Dad's heart stopped beating, it was only a matter of hours before Mother could no longer draw breath."

What a beautiful picture of oneness.

I want that kind of oneness for Norma and me. And I want it for you.

If your unity flame has dimmed over the years, fan it back into brightness. If it's burned out, get it lit again.

Avoid the five destructive winds, and protect the fire of unity and oneness with everything you've got.

If you do, you'll have a flame that will burn so brightly, everyone around you will want to know your secret. Isn't that the kind of marriage you'd like to have? And remember: a flame like that will live on in the memories of your family for generations to come.

One heart.
One love.
One flame.

CHAPTER **7**

Make a unity candle display

*N*OW THAT YOU HAVE HEARD the inspiring story of Joe and Marlene's flame and learned how to keep your own flame burning brightly, I would like to make a practical suggestion. Whether or not you had a unity candle at your wedding, I encourage you to create a unity-candle display in your home. Let the physical presence of a unity candle remind you of your priority to preserve and nurture your oneness.

It doesn't have to be a fancy candelabra. It can be merely three candles grouped together, perhaps the center candle taller than the two outside ones. Choose a separate color candle to represent each of you individually, then make the candle in the middle a color that represents a blend of the two of you. You may want to choose the blue and yellow we have used for illustration purposes in this book, or you may want to choose two other colors. The candle representing you as a couple could be the blend of your two separate colors.

I also encourage you to light the middle candle periodically to remind yourselves that you are a couple. One couple I know lights the unity candle on their six-month and yearly anniversaries. They read the Scripture passages they chose for their wedding ceremony and reflect on God's goodness. They talk about how their marriage has grown or been challenged in the past six months or year. Often these discussions lead them to ask for and receive forgiveness from each other. Sometimes the couple sets goals for the coming six months or year to set a direction for their relationship and hold each other accountable for the things they decide are important. Then they pray together and commit themselves once more to their vows and to being a couple.

Other people use the unity-candle display in their home as a conversation starter with their children and guests. The candles have sparked some fruitful discussions about the meaning of marriage and the couples' commitment to oneness.

Use your own creativity to make the unity-candle display an important reminder of your unity and an effective tool for protecting that oneness. The visual display will serve as a daily reminder that the two of you have become one. It will be a symbol of your bond and oneness.

As you continue in a deeper understanding of the unity candle, you will find yourselves making more of an effort to maintain your oneness.

Your one flame.

ABOUT THE AUTHOR

Dr. Gary Smalley, founder and chairman of the board of the Smalley Relationship Center, is one of the country's best-known authors and speakers on family relationships. He is the author and coauthor of eighteen books, including the best-selling, award-winning books *Marriage for a Lifetime, Secrets to Lasting Love, The Blessing* (with John Trent), *The Two Sides of Love* (with John Trent), and *The Language of Love* (with John Trent), as well as *Bound by Honor* (with his son Greg Smalley), and his recent release, *Food and Love.* Gary has also produced several popular films and videos.

In his thirty years of ministry Gary has spoken to more than two million people in conferences. He has been presenting his two-day work-shop "Love Is a Decision" once a month for more than twenty years. His award-winning infomercial "Hidden Keys to Loving Relationships" has been viewed by television audiences all over the world.

Several versions of the infomercial—with Dick Clark, with John Tesh and Connie Sellecca, and with Frank and Kathie Lee Gifford—have been aired.

Gary has appeared on national televisions programs such as *The Oprah Winfrey Show, Larry King Live,* the *Today* show, and *Sally Jessy Raphael,* as well as numerous national radio programs. Gary has been featured on hundreds of regional and local television and radio programs across the United States.

In addition to earning a master's degree from Bethel Theological Seminary (Minnesota), Gary has received two honorary doctorates, one from Biola University (California) and one from Southwest Baptist University (Missouri) for his work with couples.

Gary is partnering with his three grown children in ministry to married couples and families. Dr. Greg Smalley is the founder of a full-service counseling center in Branson, Missouri. Michael Smalley is a marriage therapist with a master's degree from Wheaton College Graduate School. Kari Smalley Gibson is a successful author of children's books. Gary and his wife, Norma, have been married for nearly forty years and live in Branson, Missouri. They have been blessed with eight grandchildren.

To find out more about the resources of the Smalley Relationship Center, to schedule speaking engagements, or to receive information about many marriage and family products, use these contact numbers:

The Smalley Relationship Center
1482 Lakeshore Drive
Branson, MO 65616
Phone: (417) 335-4321
Phone: (800) 84-TODAY (848-6329)
Fax: (417) 336-3515
Web site: www.smalleyonline.com